What tools do we use...?

In the garden

Vic Parker

Heinemann
LIBRARY

Little Nippers

www.heinemann.co.uk/library
Visit our website to find out more information about **Heinemann Library** books.

To order:
☎ Phone 44 (0) 1865 888066
▤ Send a fax to 44 (0) 1865 314091
▢ Visit the Heinemann Bookshop at www.heinemann.co.uk/library to browse our catalogue and order online.

First published in Great Britain by Heinemann Library, Halley Court, Jordan Hill, Oxford OX2 8EJ, part of Harcourt Education.
Heinemann is a registered trademark of Harcourt Education Ltd.

Editorial: Jilly Attwood and Louise Galpine
Design: Jo Hinton-Malivoire and bigtop, Bicester, UK
Models made by: Jo Brooker
Picture Research: Rosie Garai
Production: Séverine Ribierre

Originated by Dot Gradations
Printed and bound in China by South China Printing Company

ISBN 0 431 17152 1 (hardback)
07 06 05 04 03
10 9 8 7 6 5 4 3 2 1

ISBN 0 431 17157 2 (paperback)
07 06 05 04 03
10 9 8 7 6 5 4 3 2 1

British Library Cataloguing in Publication Data
Parker, Vic,
What tools do we use...? In the garden
635'.0284
A full catalogue record for this book is available from the British Library.

Acknowledgements
The publishers would like to thank the following for permission to reproduce photographs:
Chris Honeywell p. **23** (top right); DIY Photo Library p.**17**; Garden Picture Library p.**15** (Mel Watson); Gareth Boden pp. **5**, **6**, **7**, **8-9**, **12** (inset top right), **14**, **16**, **18-19**, **20-21**, **22-23**; Getty Images p.**10** (inset); Getty Images pp.**10** (Photomondo), **12** (Ian Shaw); Masterfile p.**11** (Matthew Wiley); NHPA p.**13** (Stephen Dalton); Trevor Clifford p.**12** (inset right).

Cover photograph reproduced with permission of Gareth Boden.

The publishers would like to thank Annie Davy for her assistance in the preparation of this book.

Contents

Digging tools 4

Planting tools 6

Weeding tools 8

Watering tools 10

Tools for building things 12

Cutting tools 14

Pond and patio tools 16

Tools for tidying 18

Tools for carrying 20

What are these garden tools? 22

Index 24

Gardening is **mUddy, mucKy** fun.

A spade is made for digging deep holes.

dig, dig, dig!

5

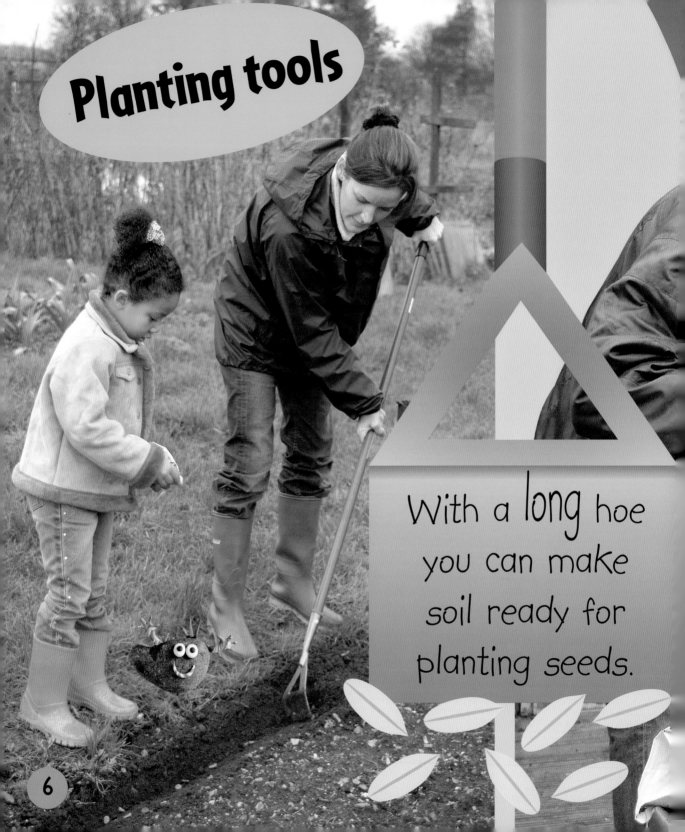

Planting tools

With a **long** hoe you can make soil ready for planting seeds.

With a small trowel you can plant flowers in **big** round tubs.

Weeding tools

This small tool is useful for pulling out weeds.

9

Watering tools

Plants need water to grow. Give them a tiny rain shower with a watering can.

A hose and sprinkler are good for watering the grass.

hose

sprinkler

Tools for building things

Wood, a saw, a hammer and some nails ...

... can make a feeding table for birds to visit.

Cutting tools

Snip!

Snip!

Shears can cut up high.

Buzz!

Buzz!

A lawn mower cuts down low.

Pond and patio tools

A fishing net is useful for scooping out **soggy** leaves.

Sometimes patios get **grimy**.

A power washer is great for blasting away **dirt**.

Tools for tidying

Tidy up leaves with a rake.

19

Tools for carrying

Take the leaves away in a wheelbarrow.

What are these garden tools?

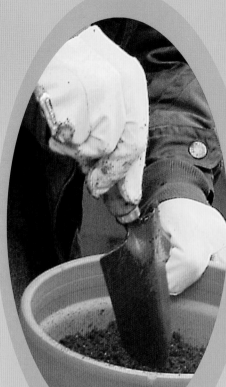

trowel

wheelbarrow

shears

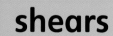

22

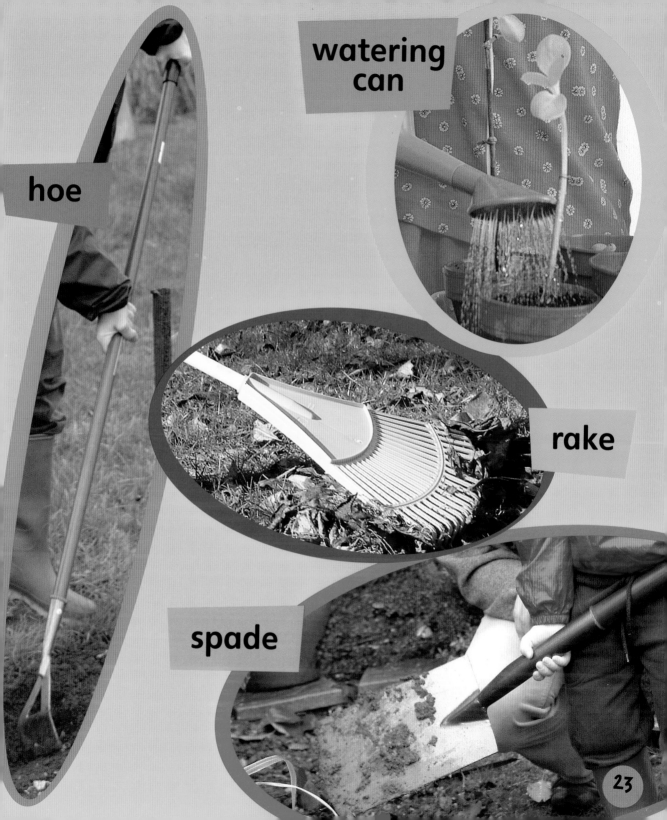

hoe

watering can

rake

spade

23

Index

broom 19

shears 14, 22

fork 9

spade 4, 23

hoe 6, 23

trowel 7, 22

rake 18, 23

wheelbarrow 20, 22

The end

Notes for adults

'What tools do we use . . .? explores a variety of tools that a young child may come across in different situations. The series encourages young children to think creatively about the different jobs these tools do, and what other tools they might use to do the same job. The books provide opportunities for discussing how the tools should be used safely and correctly, and what materials the tools are made from. There are four titles in the series: At school, At home, In the kitchen and In the garden. Used together, the books will enable comparison of similarities and differences between a wide variety of tools.

The key curriculum Early Learning Goals relevant to this series are:
• learn skills by using a range of tools
• select tools and techniques necessary to shape, assemble and join a range of materials
• talk about tools and their effects and how they work
• realize that tools can be used for a purpose and introduce children to appropriate tools
  to work on different materials
• encourage children to use the correct names for tools.

This book introduces the reader to a range of tools we use in the garden. The book will help children extend their vocabulary, as they will hear new words such as hoe and shears. You may like to introduce and explain other new words yourself, such as compost and gardener.

Additional information about tools
A tool is defined as any object which you use to perform an operation to achieve an end. Tools can be small, like pencils, or large, like lawn mowers. Tools can be hand-held, such as screwdrivers, or stationary, such as pasta-making machines. Tools can be manual, like saws, or power-driven, such as hair-dryers. Tools can be classified by their function, such as: joining things or shaping things; by their mode of operation, such as: sticking things or cleaning things; or by their mode of action, such as: tools that cut, tools that mix, tools that suck.

Follow-up activities
• Plant and care for some seeds in a flower-bed or vegetable patch, using a hoe, a trowel, a fork and
  a watering can.
• Help your child to thread some bird food onto a string, then attach it to a tree or fence using a
  hammer and nails.